EDGE BOOKS™

Kitchen Science

D1002379

Science Experiments THAT EXPLODE AND IMPLODE

Fun Projects for Curious Kids

by Jodi Wheeler-Toppen

CAPSTONE PRESS
a capstone imprint

Edge Books are published by Capstone Press,
151 Good Counsel Drive, P.O. Box 669, Mankato, Minnesota 56002.
www.capstonepub.com

Books published by Capstone Press are manufactured with paper
containing at least 10 percent post-consumer waste.

Library of Congress Cataloging-in-Publication Data
Wheeler-Toppen, Jodi.
  Science Experiments that explode and implode : fun projects for curious kids /
Jodi Wheeler-Toppen.
       p. cm.—(Edge books. Kitchen science)
  Summary: "Provides step-by-step instructions for science projects using
household materials and explains the science behind the experiments"—Provided
by publisher.
  Includes bibliographical references and index.
  ISBN 978-1-4296-5427-2 (library binding)
  ISBN 978-1-4296-6250-5 (paperback)
  1. Explosions—Experiments—Juvenile literature. 2. Pressure—Experiments—
Juvenile literature. 3. Science—Experiments—Juvenile literature. I. Title. II. Series.

QD516.W476 2011
507.8—dc22

                          2010027687

Editorial Credits
Lori Shores, editor; Veronica Correia, designer; Sarah Schuette, photo stylist;
    Marcy Morin, studio scheduler; Wanda Winch, media researcher;
    Eric Manske, production specialist

Photo Credits
All photos by Capstone Studio/Karon Dubke

Printed in the United States of America in Stevens Point, Wisconsin.
092010   005934WZS11

TABLE OF Contents

InTRODUCTION

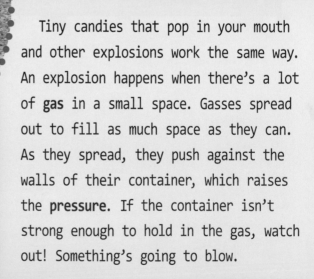

Kaboom! Nothing in science is as exciting as an explosion, except maybe an inside-out explosion. You don't have to be in a laboratory to get in on the fun. Just gather some materials in the kitchen and get to work.

Tiny candies that pop in your mouth and other explosions work the same way. An explosion happens when there's a lot of **gas** in a small space. Gasses spread out to fill as much space as they can. As they spread, they push against the walls of their container, which raises the **pressure**. If the container isn't strong enough to hold in the gas, watch out! Something's going to blow.

gas—a substance that spreads to fill any space that holds it
pressure—a force that pushes on something

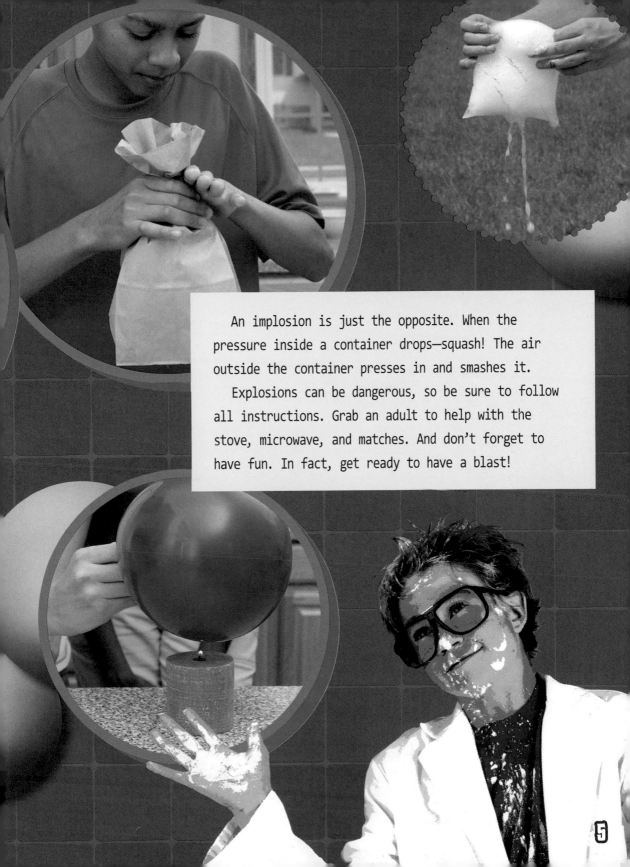

An implosion is just the opposite. When the pressure inside a container drops—squash! The air outside the container presses in and smashes it.

Explosions can be dangerous, so be sure to follow all instructions. Grab an adult to help with the stove, microwave, and matches. And don't forget to have fun. In fact, get ready to have a blast!

POWDER BURST

Here's an explosion to try the next time your family gets take-out food. Eat your meal. Then use the bag it came in to end dinner with a bang.

What you need:

- ½ cup (120 mL) cornstarch
- small paper bag

What you do:

1 Put cornstarch into a small paper bag.

You can do this experiment without the cornstarch. However, you won't be able to see the air swirling away.

2 Squeeze the neck of the bag with one hand so there is only a small hole at the top. Spread the top of the bag open so that you can blow into the hole.

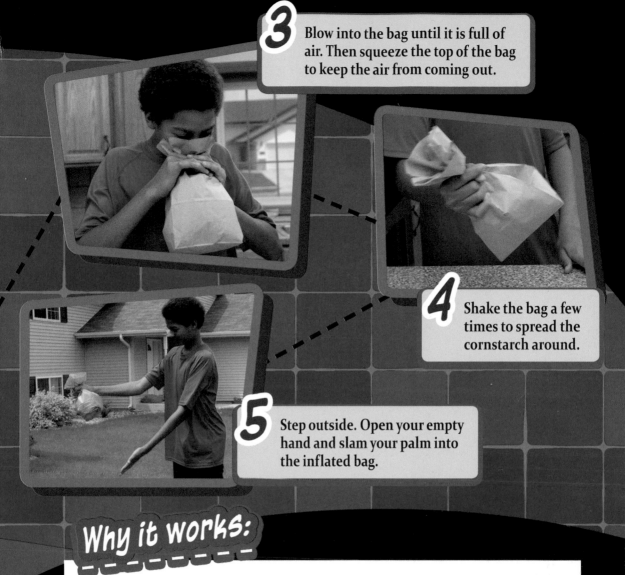

3 Blow into the bag until it is full of air. Then squeeze the top of the bag to keep the air from coming out.

4 Shake the bag a few times to spread the cornstarch around.

5 Step outside. Open your empty hand and slam your palm into the inflated bag.

Why it works:

You may think you are just popping a bag, but you are really causing an explosion. As your hand slams into the bag, the space inside the bag gets smaller. The air **molecules** inside the bag get crowded, and the pressure increases. The bag can't hold air under that much pressure. It rips, and the air escapes. The escaping air is moving quickly, which makes the air around it move too. In less than half a second, some of that speedy air hits your eardrum, and you hear the bang.

Molecule—the smallest part of an element that can exist and still keep the characteristics of the element

SLOW MOTION EXPLOSION

Some kids don't like to take baths. Here's their greatest nightmare—a bar of soap that gets bigger and bigger! Try this experiment for some good, clean fun.

What you need:

- bar of Ivory soap
- paper plate

Don't let that soap go to waste! Squish it into a ball and use it in the shower.

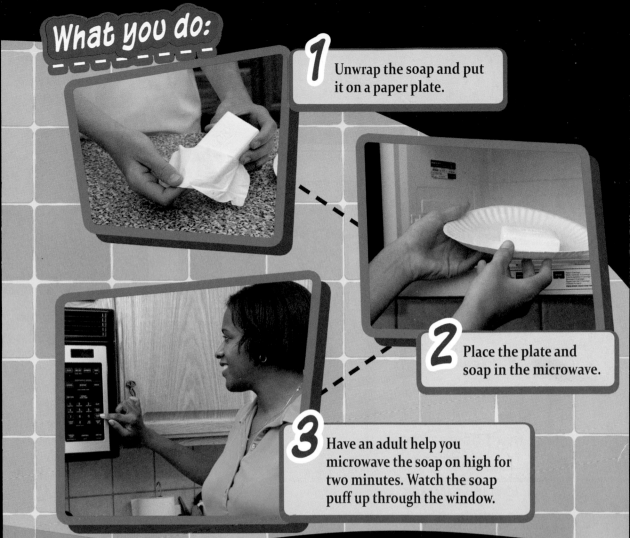

1 Unwrap the soap and put it on a paper plate.

2 Place the plate and soap in the microwave.

3 Have an adult help you microwave the soap on high for two minutes. Watch the soap puff up through the window.

Why it works:

Ivory isn't ordinary soap. It's whipped soap. When the soap is whipped, it fills with tiny pockets of air. Microwaving the soap heats up the air. Hot molecules move faster than slow molecules. As the molecules speed up, the pockets of air **expand**. The air pushes out and carries puffs of soap along with it.

expand—to increase in size

The Unpoppable Balloon

You can really make your friends squirm with this experiment. Hold a balloon over a candle and have them waiting for a bang. Surprise! You have a fireproof balloon.

What you do:

1 Start out by showing that your balloons really do pop. Blow up one balloon, and have an adult light the candle.

2 Hold the balloon over the candle. The balloon doesn't even have to touch the flame to pop.

Don't let go when you are blowing up the second balloon. You'll get drenched!

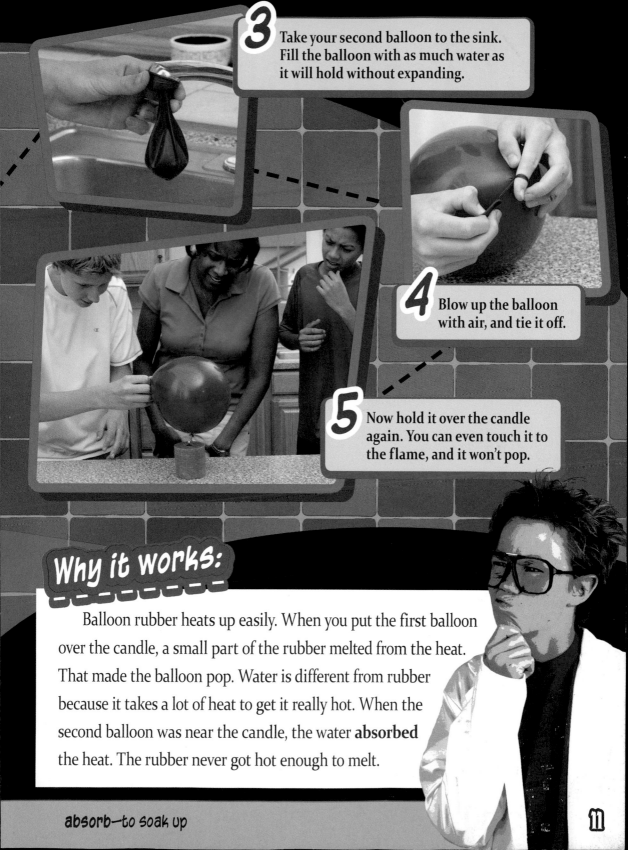

3 Take your second balloon to the sink. Fill the balloon with as much water as it will hold without expanding.

4 Blow up the balloon with air, and tie it off.

5 Now hold it over the candle again. You can even touch it to the flame, and it won't pop.

Why it works:

Balloon rubber heats up easily. When you put the first balloon over the candle, a small part of the rubber melted from the heat. That made the balloon pop. Water is different from rubber because it takes a lot of heat to get it really hot. When the second balloon was near the candle, the water **absorbed** the heat. The rubber never got hot enough to melt.

absorb—to soak up

Plastic Bag Bomb

Here's an experiment that's just bursting with excitement. Use baking soda and vinegar to create a gas in a plastic bag. The bag will swell and then explode. Head outside for the last step, or you'll have a mess to clean up!

What you need:

- toilet paper
- 2 tablespoons (30 mL) baking soda
- 1 cup (240 mL) vinegar
- zip-top plastic bag
- warm water

What you do:

1 Pull off a piece of toilet paper about two squares long. Pour baking soda onto the toilet paper.

Plastic bags with sliding zippers give the best bang.

2 Roll the toilet paper into a tube and twist the ends to hold the baking soda.

3 Pour vinegar into a zip-top plastic bag.

4 Add warm water until the bag is a little more than half full.

toilet paper

5 Carefully put the baking soda packet into the plastic bag without letting it touch the liquid. Hold it in the dry part of the bag while you zip the top.

6 Take your bag bomb outside. Let the baking soda fall into the liquid and see what happens!

Why it works:

Did you notice the bubbles in the bag? Mixing baking soda and vinegar starts a **chemical reaction** that makes carbon dioxide gas. The gas bubbles up to the surface of the liquid and then fills the top of the bag. The pressure from the gas builds up. When there is nowhere else for the gas to go, the bag bursts open and the gas escapes.

chemical reaction—a process in which one substance changes into another **13**

3-2-1 Blast Off!

Rockets use fuel explosions for power to soar into space. Build your own rocket and send it flying with the help of a fizzing antacid tablet. But don't get the tablet wet until you're ready for blast off!

What you need:

- printer paper
- 35-mm film canister
- tape
- scissors
- 1 teaspoon (5 mL) water
- fizzing antacid tablet

Most places that print photographs will give you a film canister for free if you ask.

What you do:

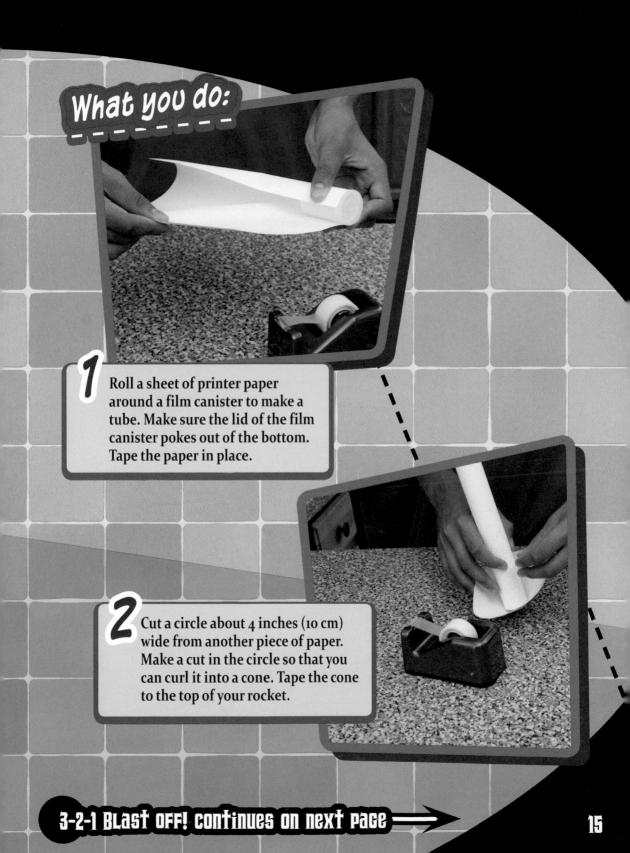

1 Roll a sheet of printer paper around a film canister to make a tube. Make sure the lid of the film canister pokes out of the bottom. Tape the paper in place.

2 Cut a circle about 4 inches (10 cm) wide from another piece of paper. Make a cut in the circle so that you can curl it into a cone. Tape the cone to the top of your rocket.

3-2-1 Blast Off! continues on next page ⟶

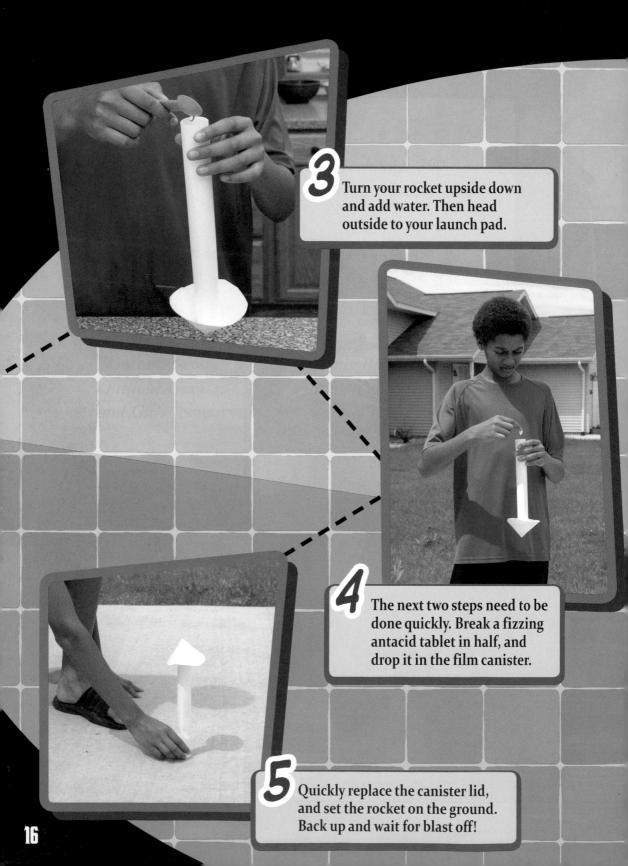

3 Turn your rocket upside down and add water. Then head outside to your launch pad.

4 The next two steps need to be done quickly. Break a fizzing antacid tablet in half, and drop it in the film canister.

5 Quickly replace the canister lid, and set the rocket on the ground. Back up and wait for blast off!

Why it works:

When you drop a fizzing antacid tablet into water, you get bubbles. The bubbles tell you that a chemical reaction is taking place. The chemical reaction makes a gas, which builds up in the film canister. The gas molecules get crowded, which raises the pressure. When the pressure gets high enough, it blows the lid off the film canister and sends the rocket flying.

It's a Gusher!

Soda pop is full of carbon dioxide gas. If you shake it, you'd better be careful when you open the lid. Shaking the soda will make those bubbles rush to the top. You can use a little candy to make an even bigger splash. But prepare to run, or you'll end up soaked!

What you need:

- printer paper
- mint-flavored Mentos candy
- tape
- 2-liter bottle of diet cola

What you do:

1 Open the bottle of diet cola, and set it on the ground.

2 Roll a sheet of printer paper into a tube that is just a little wider than the roll of candy. Tape the side so that it stays rolled up.

3 Drop six candies into the tube of paper. Pinch the tube at the end to keep the candies from sliding out.

4 Hold the tube of paper on the mouth of the bottle so the tube is standing up.

Be sure to do this activity outside. It makes a huge mess.

5 Relax your fingers so the candies slide into the bottle. Once the candies drop, run!

Why it Works:

Usually, carbon dioxide gas is spread throughout a soft drink in tiny bubbles. Only a few bubbles come to the surface at a time. In this experiment, the candy causes all of the gas to come to the top at the same time. If you looked at a Mentos mint under a microscope, you would see that it is covered with tiny bumps. The carbon dioxide bubbles collect on the bumps and join to make bigger bubbles. The big bubbles are too large to stay in the liquid. They come rushing out of the mouth of the bottle, pushing some of the soda into the air.

Egg Trap

Dropping an egg into a bottle sounds easy. But what if the egg is bigger than the mouth of the bottle? You can do it with a little help from air pressure.

What you need:

- bottle with a wide mouth
- hard-boiled egg, a little bigger than the opening of the bottle
- matches

A stage 3 baby food jar and an extra large egg work well for this activity.

What you do:

1 Peel a hard-boiled egg, and rinse it off.

2 Set the egg on the mouth of the bottle. It just sits there without moving.

3 Remove the egg from the bottle. Have an adult light four matches all at once. Ask the adult to hold the matches over the mouth of the bottle for a few seconds.

4 Have the adult drop the matches into the bottle. Quickly set the egg back on the mouth of the bottle. Watch as the egg slides into the bottle.

Why it works:

This experiment may not look like an implosion, but the science behind it is the same. The burning matches heat up the air molecules, which makes them move faster. Some of the air molecules escape out of the top of the bottle, which is why the egg wiggles a little. When the fire goes out, the air molecules cool and slow down. The pressure inside the bottle drops. But powerful air pressure pushing down on the egg squishes it right into the bottle.

21

Stink Bombs

When you mix up a batch of garlic bubbles, people will be asking, "What stinks?" You can tell them it's just the sweet smell of science.

What you need:

- 1 cup (240 mL) water
- 2 tablespoons (30 mL) dish soap
- bowl
- 1 tablespoon (15 mL) crushed garlic
- pipe cleaner

What you do:

1 Make a bubble solution by mixing water and dish soap in a bowl.

2 Add the crushed garlic to the bubble solution. Let the garlic soak for 20 minutes.

3 Twist one end of a pipe cleaner into a loop to make a bubble wand.

You can make sweet smelling bubbles by using ¼ teaspoon (1.2 mL) vanilla extract instead of garlic.

4 Dip the wand into the bubble solution, and point it toward some friends. They'll be surprised when the bubble pops and smells like garlic!

Why it works:

Plants can't run away from their enemies. But some plants have other ways to protect themselves. Garlic is one of those plants. Garlic contains tiny pockets of two odorless chemicals. When you chop garlic, or when an insect bites into it, the two chemicals mix and start a chemical reaction. The reaction makes a new chemical with a strong stink. The soap bubbles carry the smelly chemical to your friend's nose. It's strong enough to make an insect—or your friend—want to run away.

THE BiG SQUEEZE

You can squish a milk jug with just hot and cold water. Watch it swell and then shrink. It's a mini-implosion!

What you need:

- 1½ cups (360 mL) hot water
- plastic milk jug with lid
- cold water

What you do:

1 Pour hot water into an empty milk jug. Replace the lid and shake the water around for one minute.

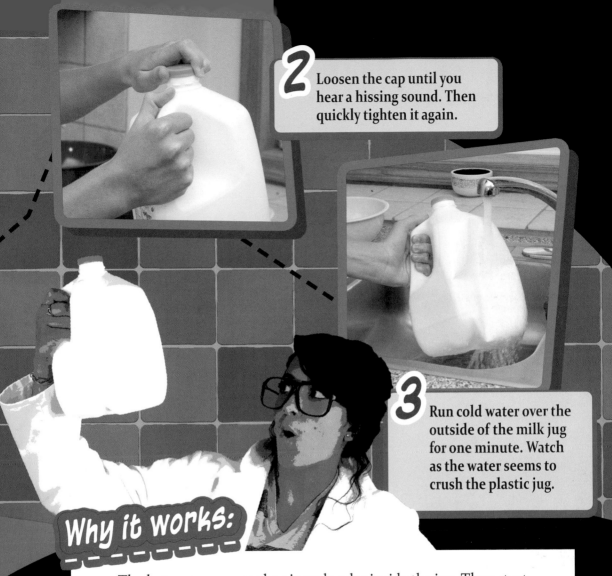

2 Loosen the cap until you hear a hissing sound. Then quickly tighten it again.

3 Run cold water over the outside of the milk jug for one minute. Watch as the water seems to crush the plastic jug.

Why it works:

The hot water warms the air molecules inside the jug. They start moving around faster. The molecules spread out and make the milk jug expand. When you loosen the lid, some of the warm air zips out. The moving air makes the hissing sound. As you run cold water over the jug, the air molecules cool off and slow down. Because some of the molecules escaped when you loosened the cap, there aren't enough left to hold up the jug's sides. The jug **contracts**.

contract—to become smaller

CRUSHED

You might not think the air in your kitchen is strong enough to smash something. But you'll be surprised. This experiment will prove that it sure can!

What you need:

- water
- an empty aluminum can
- bowl
- ice
- sauce pan
- kitchen tongs

Gather a bunch of cans before you get started. You might want to try this experiment more than once.

What you do:

1 Pour just enough water into an empty aluminum can to cover the bottom.

2 Fill a bowl with very cold water and add a few pieces of ice to keep it cold. Place the bowl next to the stove.

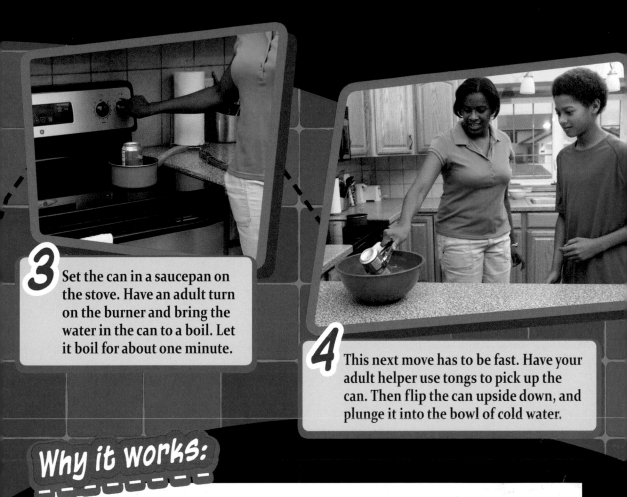

3 Set the can in a saucepan on the stove. Have an adult turn on the burner and bring the water in the can to a boil. Let it boil for about one minute.

4 This next move has to be fast. Have your adult helper use tongs to pick up the can. Then flip the can upside down, and plunge it into the bowl of cold water.

Why it works:

Air is pressing on us all the time. There's about 350 pounds (159 kg) of air pushing down on your head right now. But as long as the pressure from your insides balances out the air pressure, you don't notice. In this experiment, you make the pressure inside the soft drink can lower than the pressure outside. As the can heats up, some of the water **evaporates** into water vapor. The molecules of water vapor push the air out of the can. When the water vapor cools off in the bowl of ice water, the molecules **condense** back into liquid water. Suddenly, there's not enough gas in the can to put pressure on the sides. But there's a lot of pressure outside of the can, so you get a real smash-up job.

evaporate—to change from a liquid into a gas
condense—to change from gas to liquid

Inside-Out Balloon

If you think there's only one way to blow up a balloon, think again. In this experiment, you'll do more than just implode a balloon. You'll turn it completely inside out and inflate it backward.

What you need:

- 2 teaspoons (10 mL) water
- glass bottle, clean
- oven mitts
- balloon

What you do:

1 Pour water into the bottle.

2 Have an adult help you microwave the bottle on high for one minute. Lay the bottle on its side to make it fit in the microwave if necessary.

3 Have your adult helper use oven mitts to pull the bottle out of the microwave. Quickly stretch a balloon over the mouth of the bottle.

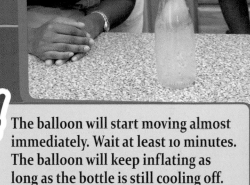

Practice stretching the balloon over the mouth of the bottle before you start. Doing so will make step 3 easier.

4 The balloon will start moving almost immediately. Wait at least 10 minutes. The balloon will keep inflating as long as the bottle is still cooling off.

Why it works:

Microwave ovens work by heating the water molecules inside your food. Since there's only water in the bottle in this experiment, the microwave gets right to work. The water molecules evaporate and spread out. They push the air molecules out of the bottle. As the bottle cools, the water vapor turns back into a liquid. Normally, air would rush back into the bottle, but this time, a balloon is in the way. So the air pushes the balloon in and inflates it in the bottle.

GLOSSARY

absorb (ab-ZORB)—to soak up

chemical reaction (KEM-uh-kuhl ree-AK-shuhn)—a process in which one substance changes into another

condense (kuhn-DENS)—to change from gas to liquid

contract (kuhn-TRAKT)—to become smaller

evaporate (i-VA-puh-rayt)—to change from a liquid into a gas

expand (ik-SPAND)—to increase in size

gas (GASS)—a substance that spreads to fill any space that holds it

molecule (MOL-uh-kyool)—the smallest part of an element that can exist and still keep the characteristics of the element

pressure (PRESH-ur)—a force that pushes on something

solution (suh-LOO-shuhn)—a mixture made up of a substance that has been dissolved in a liquid

Read More

Cobb, Vicki, and Kathy Darling. *We Dare You: Hundreds of Fun Science Bets, Challenges, and Experiments You Can Do at Home.* New York: Skyhorse Pub., 2008.

Connolly, Sean. *The Book of Totally Irresponsible Science.* New York: Workman Pub., 2008.

O'Neal, Claire. *A Project Guide to Volcanoes.* Earth Science Projects for Kids. Hockessin, Del.: Mitchell Lane Publishers, 2011.

Internet Sites

FactHound offers a safe, fun way to find Internet sites related to this book. All of the sites on FactHound have been researched by our staff.

Here's all you do:

Visit *www.facthound.com*

Type in this code: **9781429654272**

Super-cool stuff!

Check out projects, games and lots more at
www.capstonekids.com

Index